Jesus

SUPREME CONQUEROR

BILL DONAHUE

InterVarsity Press
Downers Grove, Illinois

Inter-Varsity Press
Leicester, England

InterVarsity Press, USA
P.O. Box 1400, Downers Grove, IL 60515-1426, USA
World Wide Web: www.ivpress.com
E-mail: mail@ivpress.com

Inter-Varsity Press, England
38 De Montfort Street, Leicester LE1 7GP, England
Website: www.ivpbooks.com
E-mail: ivp@ivp-editorial.co.uk

InterVarsity Press®, USA, is the book-publishing division of InterVarsity Christian Fellowship/USA®, a student movement active on campus at hundreds of universities, colleges and schools of nursing in the United States of America, and a member movement of the International Fellowship of Evangelical Students. For information about local and regional activities, write Public Relations Dept., InterVarsity Christian Fellowship/USA, 6400 Schroeder Rd., P.O. Box 7895, Madison, WI 53707-7895, or visit the IVCF website at <www.intervarsity.org>.

Inter-Varsity Press, England, is the publishing division of the Universities and Colleges Christian Fellowship (formerly the Inter-Varsity Fellowship), a student movement linking Christian Unions in universities and colleges throughout Great Britain, and a member movement of the International Fellowship of Evangelical Students. For information about local and national activities write to UCCF, 38 De Montfort Street, Leicester LE1 7GP, email us at email@uccf.org.uk, or visit the UCCF website at www.uccf.org.uk.

Design: Cindy Kiple
Images: Photodisc Collection/Getty Images

USA ISBNs 0-8308-2158-9
           978-0-8308-2158-7

UK ISBNs   1-84474-118-4
           978-1-84474-118-2

Printed in the United States of America ∞

| P | 91 | 18 | 17 | 16 | 15 | 14 | 13 | 12 | 11 | 10 | 9 | 8 | 7 | 6 | 5 | 4 | 3 | 2 |
| Y | 19 | 18 | 17 | 16 | 15 | 14 | 13 | 12 | 11 | | | | | | | | | |

CONTENTS

CONTENTS

BEFORE YOU BEGIN

The Jesus 101 series is designed to help you respond to Jesus as you encounter him in the stories and teachings of the Bible, particularly the Gospel accounts of the New Testament. The "101" designation does not mean "simple"; it means "initial." You probably took introductory-level courses in high school or at a university, like Economics 101 or Biology 101. Each was an initial course, a first encounter with the teachings and principles of the subject matter. I had my first encounter with economic theory in Econ 101, but it was not necessarily simple or always easy (at least not for me!).

Jesus 101 may be the first time you looked closely at Jesus. For the first time you will encounter his grace and love, be exposed to his passion and mission, and get a firsthand look at the way he connects with people like you and me. Or perhaps, like me, you have been a Christian many years. In that case you will encounter Jesus for the first time all over again. Often when I read a biblical account of an event in Jesus' life, even if the text is very familiar to me, I am amazed at a new insight or a fresh, personal connection with Jesus I hadn't experienced before.

I believe Jesus 101 will challenge your thinking and stir your soul regardless of how far along the spiritual pathway you might be. After all, Jesus is anything but dull: he tended to shake up the world of everyone who interacted with him. Sometimes people sought him out; often he surprised them. In every case, he challenged them, evoking a reaction they could hardly ignore.

There are many ways we might encounter Jesus. In this series we will focus on eight. You will come face to face with Jesus as

- Provocative Teacher
- Sacred Friend
- Extreme Forgiver
- Authentic Leader
- Truthful Revealer
- Compassionate Healer
- Relentless Lover
- Supreme Conqueror

☐ HOW THESE GUIDES ARE PUT TOGETHER

In each of the discussion guides you will find material for six group meetings, though feel free to use as many meetings as necessary to cover the material. That is up to you. Each group will find its way. The important thing is to encounter and connect with Christ, listen to what he is saying, watch what he is doing—and then personalize that encounter individually and as a group.

The material is designed to help you engage with one another, with the Bible and with the person of Jesus. The experiences below are designed to guide you along when you come together as a group.

Gathering to Listen

This short section orients you to the material by using an illustration, a quote or a text that raises probing questions, makes provocative assumptions or statements, or evokes interpersonal tension or thoughtfulness. It may just make you laugh. It sets the tone for the dialogue you will be having together. Take a moment here to connect with one another and focus your attention on the reading. Listen carefully as thoughts and emotions are stirred.

After the reading, you will have an opportunity to respond in some way. What are your first impressions, your assumptions, disagreements, feelings? What comes to mind as you read this?

Encountering Jesus

Here you meet Jesus as he is described in the Bible text. You will encounter his teachings, his personal style and his encounters with people much like you. This section will invite your observations, questions and initial reactions to what Jesus is saying and doing.

Joining the Conversation

A series of group questions and interactions will encourage your little community to engage with one another about the person and story of Jesus. Here you will remain for a few moments in the company of Jesus and of one another. This section may pose a question about your group or ask you to engage in an exercise or interaction with one another. The goal is to discover a sense of community as you question and discover what God is doing.

Connecting Our Stories

Here you are invited to connect your story (life, issues, questions, challenges) with Jesus' story (his teaching, character and actions). We look at our background and history, the things that encourage or disappoint us. We seek to discover what God is doing in our life and the lives of others, and we develop a sense of belonging and understanding.

Finding Our Way

A final section of comments and questions invites you to investigate next steps for your spiritual journey as a group and personally. It will evoke and prompt further action, decisions or conversations in response to what was discovered and discussed. You will prompt one another to listen to God more deeply, take relational risks and invite God's work in your group and in the community around you.

Praying Together

God's Holy Spirit is eager to teach you! Remember that learning is not just a mental activity; it involves relationship and action. One educator suggests that all learning is the result of failed expectations. We hope, then, that at some point your own expectations will fail, that you will be ambushed by the truth and stumble into new and unfamiliar territory that startles you into new ways of thinking about God and relating to him through Christ. And so prayer—talking and listening to God—is a vital part of the Jesus 101 journey.

If you are seeking to discover Jesus for the first time, your prayer can be a very simple expression of your thoughts and questions to God. It may include emotions like anger, frustration, joy or wonder. If you already have an intimate, conversational relationship with God, your prayer will reflect the deepest longings and desires of your soul. Prayer is an integral part of the spiritual life, and small groups are a great place to explore it.

☐ **HOW DO I PREPARE?**

No preparation is required! Reading the Bible text ahead of time, if you can, will provide an overview of what lies ahead and will give you an opportunity to reflect on the Bible passages. But you will not feel out of the loop or penalized in some way if you do not get to it. This material is designed for *group* discovery and interaction. A sense of team and community develops and excitement grows as you explore the material together. In contrast to merely discussing what everyone has already discovered prior to the meeting, "discovery in the moment" evokes a sense of shared adventure.

If you want homework, do that after each session. Decide how you might face your week, your job, your relationships and family in light of what you have just discovered about Jesus.

☐ A FINAL NOTE

These studies are based on the book *In the Company of Jesus*. It is not required that you read the book to do any Jesus 101 study—each stands alone. But you might consider reading the parallel sections of the book to enrich your experience between small group meetings. The major sections of the book take up the same eight ways that we encounter Jesus in the Jesus 101 guides. So the eight guides mirror the book in structure and themes, but the material in the book is not identical to that of the guides.

Jesus 101 probes more deeply into the subject matter, whereas *In the Company of Jesus* is designed for devotional and contemplative reading and prayer. It is filled with stories and anecdotes to inspire and motivate you in your relationship with Christ.

I pray and hope that you enjoy this adventure as you draw truth from the Word of God for personal transformation, group growth and living out God's purposes in the world!

THE SUPREME CONQUEROR

In high school my brother was a competitive swimmer. Fortunately, his teams were strong and won a number of meets. After each meet he'd come through the door at home, and we'd ask the same question: "Did you guys win today?" If not, his response was always the same. "No, we came in second."

It was his funny way of making light of the loss. He still talks that way today when his favorite football team loses a game: "They came in second."

When you run a marathon against a hundred others, second is pretty impressive. But in many sporting contests, second place is unacceptable. (Gladiators knew this well!)

Everyone likes a winner in business, athletics, game shows and politics. And Americans tend to be especially enthusiastic when the underdog beats the odds-on favorite. When a marketing representative helps close the deal and drive off competitors, the boss is ecstatic. When our kids do well at ballet class or at the recital, we burst with pride. And when a graduate student aces her final exams and graduates at the top of her class—it's time to party! Winning is something we are trained to strive for.

Of course, sometimes winning is sheer luck, as when golfer Tiger Woods dropped in a sixty-foot chip shot from the rough on the sixteenth hole at the 2005 Masters Tournament. Without that shot, he probably would never have held on to force a sudden-death playoff. He defeated Chris DiMarco on the first hole of that playoff. DiMarco did walk away with over $750,000 in prize money—second place in professional golf has its rewards. But we all knew he would rather have been wearing the green Masters jacket given to the winner each year.

Jesus is a winner—but in a much different sense. His strategy was countercultural, his methods unorthodox, his victory otherworldly. The Bible describes him as a conquering hero—but a hero who had to die first. Ask most military leaders if that's a good strategy. World War II commander George Patton was famous for saying, "No one ever won a war dying for his country. You win a war by making the other guy die for his country!" Patton's actual language was more colorful, but you get the idea.

It is counterintuitive to defeat death by dying or to accomplish your mission by allowing the enemy to have his way with you. It just doesn't make sense. In our world conquering heroes achieve victory by force, not submission; with power, not weakness; with superior weapons and troops, not alone and empty handed. But Jesus conquered through weakness, submission and death. And his death rocked the world and defeated the one who seeks to destroy all that is good.

Unorthodox? Unusual? Unconventional? Yes, yes, yes.

Unsuccessful? Quite the contrary. Jesus is the Supreme Conqueror, and we can all be eternally grateful not simply for what he did but for how he chose to do it.

ONE

CONFRONTS OUR ENEMY

Get behind me, Satan.

☐ GATHERING TO LISTEN

When an enemy is too tough to handle or too big to topple, it's nice to have some help. The "enemy" may be an opposing player, a neighborhood bully or a social calamity that threatens to defeat us.

William Booth, famed founder of the Salvation Army, was in an exasperated state when his son, Bramwell, arrived for a visit one morning. William had arrived back in London late the night before, after traveling to a town in southern England. What he had seen that evening had inflamed his passion and stirred his soul. "Bramwell," cried William to his son, "did you know that men slept out all night on the bridges?"

"Well, yes," replied Bramwell to his father, "a lot of poor fellows, I suppose, do that."

"Then you ought to be ashamed of yourself to have known it and have done nothing for them," William admonished him. Bramwell listed a number of factors that would make addressing the problem difficult, but his father was not moved. "Go and do something! Give them some shelter. Get a warehouse; warm it up. Something must be done!" And so began the Salvation Army shelters.

Soon the hands of many joined in, and the vision became a reality. Countless poor men, homeless and with no power to change their condition, were helped by the Booths and their shelters.

Poverty, an enemy in any culture, cannot be defeated by the poor. They need help. Someone must confront this foe on their behalf, helping them to battle back and build a normal life.

Bramwell later said of his father, "The horizon of his soul was not limited by human hope—it reached out to Divine Power and Love." William Booth needed God's power to confront the enemy of poverty, and the poor men who slept on the bridges needed Booth. When an enemy seems overwhelming, we need someone to help us confront it.

- Have you ever been part of a team or group that fought against injustice? Or have you ever had to step in and defend the powerless or the weak? What was that like?

☐ **ENCOUNTERING JESUS**

Jesus is unafraid of the enemies that threaten us and our world. He is more than willing to confront and defeat them. However, not everyone is pleased when he does so.

Read Luke 8:26-39.

1. Describe the condition of the man Jesus meets. What is your first reaction to him? (Try to imagine his appearance as he meets Jesus.)

2. One of the most intriguing aspects of this story is the varying responses to what Jesus does. What do you notice about how the demons address Jesus? What does this "legion" believe and understand about Jesus?

   What is the reaction of the pig herders?

   What is the response of the eyewitnesses and the townspeople?

   What is the response of the demon-possessed man after he is healed?

3. What is significant about the instructions Jesus gives the man in verse 39?

Demons are spiritual beings hostile to both God and men. They opposed the teaching of Jesus and sought to destroy people. In the New Testament, we find people possessed by demons who suffer from epilepsy, loss of speech and self-mutilation. The Gospels distinguish between sickness and demon possession, calling them by name. Possession by demons is a worldwide phenomenon and should not be simply dismissed as a psychological disorder. Spiritual power is always required to confront and remove these evil beings.

☐ JOINING THE CONVERSATION

4. Have you ever encountered someone like this or seen a person who appeared mentally disturbed and disheveled? What thoughts crossed your mind?

5. Why did these people fear the power of God?

Why do *we* often fear the power of God?

☐ CONNECTING OUR STORIES

6. In what ways are our responses to God's work sometimes like these townspeople's?

Why do we have such reactions?

7. How has Jesus confronted a great enemy for you, intervening to restore or help you in ways you could not help yourself?

☐ FINDING OUR WAY

8. Jesus has the power to confront the enemy—the evil one—as he tries to destroy our families, relationships and connection with God. For

some of us the battle is intense; for others it is more subtle. God offers
to help us in engaging the enemy. What might that help look like?

9. Jesus called some to follow him and share in his ministry. Others he
   sent back into the marketplace or into the community (like this man)
   to be his witnesses. Where might he be sending you, and what is the
   story he wants you to tell?

☐ **PRAYING TOGETHER**

Thank God for sending Jesus to confront the powers of darkness and
evil that threaten to weaken us and destroy the world. Pray for courage
to face the enemy, knowing that in Christ you are neither alone nor
powerless.

TWO

Jesus

PROVIDES OUR STRATEGY

Go, I am sending you out like lambs among wolves.

☐ GATHERING TO LISTEN

What's up with God? you ask yourself. When he wants to topple a city wall in Jericho, he tells people to march around it seven times and blow trumpets. When he wants to defeat an imposing army of Midianites, Amalekites and others, he commands Gideon to reduce his troops from twenty thousand men to three hundred. When nine-foot Goliath threatens Israel, God sends a small shepherd boy with a sling and a few stones. Sure, I would have done that myself. Right.

No strategies like these would ever find their way into the situation room at the Pentagon or the war room of a battleship. Such methods make no sense—except to God. When Jesus sends his young, inexperienced followers out into a hostile world, it looks as if he's sending lambs to the slaughterhouse, a virtual mass suicide. Yet this strategy is precisely the one needed to produce the results Jesus desired.

• Assume for a moment that you are launching a new product into the marketplace. What would you want to know and what resources would you like to have to ensure a successful launch?

☐ ENCOUNTERING JESUS

Preparation is essential in any endeavor. Jesus wanted his inner circle to be clear about their mission, the resources at their disposal and the price for success as he defined it. So he gave the Twelve some instructions so they would be clear about the strategy.

Read Matthew 10:5-20.

1. Jesus gives specific instructions to the twelve apostles. What is your first response to these instructions?

2. Let's break Jesus' instructions down a bit, analyzing them in detail. The categories below may help. What strikes you about these details?

   • what to take and what
     to leave behind

   • what to say

   • what to do

   • what to do if the message
     is received or rejected

   • what to watch out for

- what treatment to expect
  from those in power

- what to say and not say
  when questioned

- what to expect in the way of a
  reward (see verses 40-42)

3. What does Jesus tell the Twelve in order to build their confidence as
   they head out?

☐ JOINING THE CONVERSATION

4. Every mission worth achieving has a strategy behind it; it will not be
   accomplished through a series of haphazard, random initiatives.
   What are some of the elements of a good strategy?

5. What disturbs you about what Jesus has said?

Does it seem unfair for them to be sent to Israel (where they would relate to other Jews) first?

☐ CONNECTING OUR STORIES

6. Have you ever been sent on a mission, either at work or in school? Explain what the objective was and how you planned to accomplish it.

7. As you consider following Jesus, either at a deeper level of commitment or for the first time, how would you describe the characteristics Jesus is looking for in his followers?

☐ FINDING OUR WAY

8. Discipleship means that Christ followers let Jesus shape the strategy, which may require a step of faith, especially when his instructions seem unreasonable, unnecessary or even counterproductive. Are there areas of life where such a step is difficult to take right now?

9. What does it mean for you to be wise as a serpent but gentle as a dove as you practice the ways of Jesus and fulfill the mission he has given?

☐ **PRAYING TOGETHER**

To yield to the strategic plan of Jesus requires humility and faith. Pray that you will grow in these two qualities, trusting Jesus' plan even if it does not seem to make sense. Remember that God uses the foolish things of this world system to confound the wise (Luke 10:21; 1 Corinthians 1:27-29) and that his ways are higher than our ways (Isaiah 55:8).

THREE

CHOOSES OUR WEAPONS

These only come out by prayer.

☐ GATHERING TO LISTEN

My father was a schoolteacher in a tough Philadelphia neighborhood, and on occasion he served as school disciplinarian. One day he received a phone call from a classroom pleading for immediate help. The caller said a student was holding a knife and threatening other students and the teacher.

A former college heavyweight wrestler who stood six feet two inches tall and weighed 250 pounds, Dad was an imposing figure. Now he grabbed a large book and a nine-inch knife he had taken from a student earlier in the week and headed to the classroom. Placing the blade inside the book, he walked through the door and into the tense situation.

"Stand back, Mr. Donahue—I have a knife and I'll use it!" called out the aggressor.

"I understand," said my dad, "but first it would be helpful for you to learn a lesson from a book I've brought. Remember, this is a school. This book has an important lesson inside for you. Can I show you what's in the book?"

Nervously, the puzzled student waved the three-inch pocketknife he held in his hand. "Okay, I guess. Show me the book."

My father opened the book, displaying the large knife with the nine-inch blade. The student's eyes widened. "Now you have a choice," counseled my father. "You can use what's in your hand, but that means I will have to use what's in the book. Or you can put your knife away, and I can close the book."

Though my dad had no intention of using the knife, he knew it would serve as a good object lesson. The aggressive student relented. The lesson was over.

One key to winning a battle is having the right weapons. The group with the strongest arsenal has a distinct advantage over others.

- Have you ever been in a situation where "weapons" determined the outcome of a conflict? Perhaps it was a superior product, a bigger athlete or a piece of technology that gave you an advantage over competitors. Describe your "weapon" to the group.

☐ ENCOUNTERING JESUS

Read Mark 9:14-29.

1. This man is desperate, and the disciples have failed to help him. Describe Jesus' reaction. Why is he so frustrated?

2. This story has some similar elements to last session's account. What do you notice about the condition of this boy while he is possessed by an evil spirit?

3. Verses 23-24 are the turning point in the story. How is Jesus testing the man and teaching the crowd?

4. As you read verses 25-29, there appears to be a contradiction. Jesus commands the spirit to come out but tells the disciples that such spirits come out only by prayer. Has Jesus prayed? What is going on here?

☐ JOINING THE CONVERSATION

5. What do you believe about the practice and power of prayer? Look over the list below and circle all that apply.
   - I pray at meals and with my kids at bedtime, but that's about it.
   - I pray when I am faced with a challenge at work or with my health.
   - I pray for others when they need help.
   - I pray for my family and friends.
   - I pray for my enemies.
   - I pray for my spiritual growth and for God's strength.
   - I pray more than once a day, not including mealtimes.
   - My prayer time has increased over the years.
   - Prayer is a new experience for me, and I need a lot of help.
   - I am consistently seeking new ways to pray.

- I pray with others.
- I believe God can and will respond to my prayers.
- I keep praying even when I do not see God at work.
- After a while, if what I've been praying for hasn't happened, I stop asking for God to intervene, assuming he just doesn't want to.
- I do not pray much at all anymore.
- I hear God speak to me when I pray.
- Prayer is enjoyable, and I find myself spending lots of time praying.
- I pray for the abolition of poverty.
- I pray for justice when I see oppression.
- I pray that healing will take place between governments who are at war.

What does this exercise reflect about your beliefs?

6. Look again at verses 23-24. What do you learn from this exchange with Jesus?

☐ **CONNECTING OUR STORIES**

7. Take a moment to identify your own areas of unbelief. There are some categories on page 28 to help prompt your thinking. In what situations or areas do you feel a lot like the man in verse 23?

- finances
- career
- your children
- relationships
- health
- your spiritual growth
- your ability to break a harmful habit or sin pattern
- organizational or church conflicts
- the potential for reconciliation where racial hatred exists

8. Tell about a time when God responded powerfully to a prayer you prayed for others or for yourself.

When your church or group prays together, God is present and his people are present. United prayer includes a visible union (people gathered together) and an agreement of mind and heart—the kind of agreement we seek in agreeing with God in our requests. That kind of praying comes about only through the leading of the Holy Spirit. When you agree with God in prayer, your request will be answered.

T. W. HUNT AND CLAUDE V. KING,
In God's Presence

☐ FINDING OUR WAY

9. The prayer of faith is easy to talk about but hard to develop. How can you encourage one another to persevere in "believing prayer" even when the odds are against you and results are not evident? Remember, prayer is a strong weapon Jesus has given us to battle the evil we face in this world.

☐ PRAYING TOGETHER

Sometimes the prayer "Lord, I believe—help my unbelief!" is most appropriate. This may be a time to stretch your faith and take some risks in prayer.

FOUR

Jesus

SUPPLIES OUR STRENGTH

I have given you power and authority.

□ **GATHERING TO LISTEN**

There are few on-the-job frustrations more irritating than to be given responsibility without resources and authority. You may have the right title on your office door, and you may have a great job description outlining your objectives, reporting relationships and responsibilities. But no one can achieve the expected results for any organization without the authority to act and the resources (the power) to make those intended actions a reality.

I worked for a bank three years after college. After twelve months of training, I was assigned to a lending officer to help him build our loan business. For three months, I analyzed financial statements, tracked lending activity and reviewed our portfolio. Occasionally, I was invited to a lunch or an event with some customers.

Soon I was given the responsibility for business expansion into New Jersey and parts of the Philadelphia area. As I contacted new customers and began to evaluate their potential for becoming a client, I found my hands tied. Potential customers wanted to know how much they could borrow, but I had no authority to make a loan over $10,000—which is nothing for a business seeking $3 million in capital. I had to call my boss and get permission to initiate a serious conversation about lending money. Yet he was often away and unavailable. Later, he chastised me for not building a larger client base.

The situation was awkward. I was responsible to create a larger lending portfolio, but I was not given the support or authority to even begin serious conversations with potential clients. As a result, clients saw me as a middle man who stood in the way. They wanted to talk with a "real" lender who had authority, so they began ignoring my calls. It was the most frustrating working environment I had ever experienced.

- What has been your most profound experience—at work or elsewhere—with a lack of power?

□ ENCOUNTERING JESUS
Read Matthew 28:16-20; Acts 1:1-8.

1. In Matthew 28:16-20 Jesus commissions his followers to go into the world and teach people his ways and message. What is the relationship between authority, power and responsibility in this commission?

2. In Acts 1 Jesus supplies the disciples with power. What kind of power is this?

How will it help them achieve their mission?

3. These verses describe a new relationship between Jesus and his followers. What does this change mean for their ministry?

4. All three Persons of the Trinity—Father, Son and Holy Spirit—are mentioned in both of these passages. What significance does each play in supplying the disciples with what they need?

☐ JOINING THE CONVERSATION

5. Knowing what you do about the eleven apostles (disciples), what might be going through their minds as Jesus commands them to go into the entire world without him?

6. In Acts 1:8 it is clear that power comes from the Spirit. What do you

think it was like to *wait* for the Holy Spirit to come? What would be on your mind?

☐ **CONNECTING OUR STORIES**

7. Jesus provides his followers with what they need to do the ministry he has given them. If you can, talk about what you think your ministry is at this point in your spiritual life.

8. What resources has he given you to accomplish that ministry?

☐ **FINDING OUR WAY**

9. Jesus delegates power and authority to the Eleven and ultimately to all of his followers. What does that mean for your group?

Where does your group need to act on the power and authority of Christ? Here are some possibilities:

- spreading the message of Jesus
- serving to meet needs in the community
- praying for the sick
- helping each other face trials
- supporting a missionary family
- bringing strength to a failing marriage
- mentoring young men and/or women

10. Some Christians are tempted to abuse or misuse the authority they have been given. How would you know if this was happening in your life or group, and how can you protect against it?

☐ **PRAYING TOGETHER**

Spend some time asking God to supply the spiritual power you need for facing the needs you have identified. He has already supplied all believers with his Holy Spirit. How aware are we of the Spirit's power, and how often do we ask God to release that power in us by faith? This is a good time to talk and pray about the authority and power we have been given.

FIVE

SECURES OUR VICTORY

Take heart, for I have overcome the world.

☐ GATHERING TO LISTEN

The sacrificial death of Christ on the cross is the foundation stone of the Christian faith. The gospel is the good news that because of the cross, we can be reconciled to God, who we have been alienated from. There is forgiveness of sin and a restored relationship with him through Jesus. We are made free at the cross and begin the process of becoming whole again.

There is power in the cross. At the cross Jesus made certain our victory over death and sin. Because he lives, we too shall live. Death is defeated, and sin is no longer the ruling force in our lives. Soon the entire world will be redeemed, and we who believe in Jesus by faith will join him, sharing in his rule over a new heaven and new earth. As a community we will come together as stewards of this new creation. The future is bright, but only because of a very dark moment on a Friday at Golgotha almost 2,000 years ago.

Jesus is the conqueror whose power has overcome the darkness of the world.

Power, then, takes its clearest meaning from the central fact of salvation—Jesus' crucifixion. It is the freedom that Jesus gives to his disciples, to let go of all that hinders a life of sacrificial love. It is the use of gifts and possessions given by God in serving the spiritual and material needs of others. It is the conquest of internal and external forces (temptation, sin and evil), which cause us to be in bondage to falsehoods and unbelief, and to destructive and oppressive spiritual, moral, intellectual, emotional, political and social influences (J. A. Kirk, "Power," in *New Dictionary of Theology*).

- How do you respond to this definition of power?
- How does this definition compare to the way our culture might define power?

☐ **ENCOUNTERING JESUS**

Read John 12:20-36.

1. In your own words, summarize what Jesus says about his sacrificial death and the impact it will have on the world.

2. Jesus appears to have a great deal of certainty about his future. He knows that victory is certain. What gives him this certainty?

3. What do you observe about how Jesus feels as he faces the reality of his impending death?

How do others respond to this?

4. What does Jesus mean by "Put your trust in the light while you have it"?

☐ JOINING THE CONVERSATION

5. There is a lot of talk about death and dying here. How do you react to the teaching that followers of Jesus must lose their life in order to truly find life?

6. Jesus said that "the prince of this world" (that is, the evil one) will be driven out. How might this encourage his followers?

☐ CONNECTING OUR STORIES

7. Jesus alludes to a spiritual battle that is ongoing. Has such a battle

ever seemed to break into your awareness and your life?

When are you most aware of it?

8. Using the chart below, compare what one's life looks like when one walks in darkness and when one walks in the light. Based on the categories on the left, choose a few adjectives or phrases for each.

	Walking in the Light	Walking in Darkness
Relationship to God		
Friendships		
View of evil		
Response to suffering		
Attitude toward work		
Use of money		
Regard for opposite sex		
Desire for power		

☐ FINDING OUR WAY

9. Knowing that at the cross Christ set us free and secured our victory over sin and death, how do you want to live?

☐ PRAYING TOGETHER

Take time to worship and be grateful. The work has been done, and the power is available for us. Pray for others who may not have this power or this certainty. Pray that God will open their eyes to see what Christ has done for them and what this means for their life.

SIX

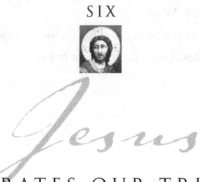

CELEBRATES OUR TRIUMPH

I saw Satan fall like lightning.

☐ GATHERING TO LISTEN

Everyone likes a good party, particularly if it is thrown in their honor! It's just not as much fun to celebrate alone.

For my wife's fortieth birthday we enjoyed a weekend in Wisconsin, finishing the time with a private horseback ride through rolling hills. As we were finishing the ride, we paused to relax a moment, but my horse caught sight of the barn. Suddenly he broke into a full gallop. Caught off guard by his sudden spurt, I was off balance in the saddle. I tried to recover but fell from the horse and punctured a lung. So much for the birthday celebration! In a few weeks I was fine, but the celebration had ended prematurely.

I decided to make up for it the next year. Gail was to meet a few friends in the upper room of a local coffee shop a week after her birthday (which we had intentionally barely acknowledged, much to her chagrin). She arrived without expectations and was quite surprised by the decorations, the presents and the hats everyone was wearing. I wanted to take part in the celebration without spoiling the fun of this "ladies-only" event. So I had concocted a surprise of my own, and only two of the women knew about it.

Gail had grown up in Central America at a time when local TV was limited to old American reruns. Her favorite show was *Zorro*, whose protagonist was the Latino version of Robin Hood. For her surprise party, I rented a black cape, a hat, black tights and a mask. With my guitar over my shoulder and a rose in my teeth, I stepped into the room. Everyone laughed until they cried as I sang a song I had written for Gail, set to the *Zorro* theme. Yes, I looked foolish. But it sure beat falling off a horse!

• Tell about the most exciting party you ever attended.

☐ ENCOUNTERING JESUS

Celebration is a spiritual discipline, a practice of pausing to honor the work of God in our lives and to encourage one another. Jesus enjoyed parties and took time to celebrate the work of God.

Read Luke 10:16-24.

1. When the Seventy-two return from a ministry adventure, Jesus celebrates their victory. What specifically does he focus on as he celebrates with them?

2. What is Jesus excited about in verse 21?

3. Jesus puts the work of the disciples in perspective and uses the celebration as a time to connect them to the greater work of God in the world. How does he do this, and why is it important?

☐ JOINING THE CONVERSATION

4. Imagine yourself as a disciple. You have just preached, healed and cast out demons. Now you are telling Jesus the story of your ministry success. Describe what you are thinking and feeling.

Joy is our portion in his fellowship. Joy goes with all confidence and creativity. It is his joy, and that is not a small joy or a repressed "joy." It is a robust joy, with no small element of outright hilarity in it. For nothing less than joy can sustain us in the kingdom righteousness that possesses us, which truly is a weighty and powerful thing to bear. It was not for nothing that Mother Teresa of Calcutta required her sisters of charity to be people who smile.

DALLAS WILLARD, *The Divine Conspiracy*

5. Jesus celebrates the revelation of the Father though the Son. Why is this significant for the seventy-two who have just returned?

☐ **CONNECTING OUR STORIES**

6. Has there ever been a time when God worked in you and it caused you to see Jesus more clearly?

7. Jesus says that those who reject his followers reject him, and those who listen to his followers listen to him. What does it mean to speak for Jesus as his representative?

☐ **FINDING OUR WAY**

8. "The harvest is plentiful," said Jesus before he sent out the seventy-two. How does knowing this influence the way you go into the world as Jesus' representative?

9. How can your group bring a spirit of celebration to your gatherings? What kinds of things could you celebrate?

☐ **PRAYING TOGETHER**

Make a list of the things God has done in you personally, in your group and through you in the lives of others. Take time to acknowledge them and celebrate them! Pray, thanking God for his great work.

NOTES FOR LEADERS

Each session has a similar format using the components below. Here is a very rough guide for the amount of time you might spend on each segment for a ninety-minute meeting time, excluding additional social time. This is a general guide, and you will learn to adjust the format as you become comfortable working together as a group:

Gathering to Listen	5-10 minutes
Encountering Jesus	15 minutes
Joining the Conversation	20 minutes
Connecting Our Stories	20 minutes
Finding Our Way	10 minutes
Praying Together	about 10 minutes

You can take some shortcuts or take longer as the group decides, but strive to stay on schedule for a ninety-minute meeting including prayer time. You will also want to save time to attend to personal needs and prayer. This will vary by group and can also be accomplished in personal relationships you develop between meetings.

As group leader, know that you help create an environment for spiritual growth. Here are a few things to consider as you invite people to follow in the company of Jesus.

LEADER TIPS

Practice authenticity and truth telling. Do not pretend an elephant is not sitting in the middle of the room when everyone knows it is.

- Does your group have a commitment to pursue personal change and growth?
- Set some ground rules or a covenant for group interactions. Consider values like confidentiality, respect and integrity.
- Model and encourage healthy self-disclosure through icebreakers, storytelling and getting to know one another between meetings.

CONNECTING SEEKERS TO JESUS

This simple process is designed to help you guide a person toward commitment to Christ. It is only a guide, intended to give you the feel of a conversation you might have.

1. *Describe what you see going on.* "Mike, I sense you are open to knowing Jesus more personally. Is this the case?"

2. *Affirm that Jesus is always inviting people to follow him (John 6:35-40).* "Mike, Jesus has opened the door to a full and dynamic relationship with him. All who believe in Jesus are welcome. Do you want to place your trust in Jesus?"

3. *Describe how sin has separated us from God, making a relationship with God impossible (Romans 3:21-26).* "Though Jesus desires fellowship with us, our sin stands in the way. So Jesus went to the cross to pay for that sin, to take away the guilt of that sin and to make reconciliation with God possible again. Are you aware that your sin has become a barrier between you and Jesus?"

4. *Show how Jesus' death on the cross bridged the gap between us and God (Romans 5:1-11).* "Now we can have peace with God, a relationship with Jesus, because his death canceled out our sin debt. All our offenses against God are taken away by Jesus."

5. *Invite them to have a brief conversation with God (2 Corinthians 5:11—6:2).* "By asking for his forgiveness and being reconnected to Jesus, we can have new life, one that starts now. Jesus invites you to join him in this new life—to love him, learn his ways, connect to his people and trust in his purposes. We can talk to him now and express that desire if you want to."

These five suggestions are designed to create a dialogue and discern if a person wants to follow Jesus. Points to remember:

1. Keep it authentic and conversational.
2. God is at work here—you are simply a guide, leading someone toward a step of faith in Jesus.
3. The heart is more important than the specific words.
4. People will not understand all that Christ has done, so don't try to confuse them with too much information.
5. Keep it simple.
6. Don't put words in someone's mouth. Let them describe how they want to follow Jesus and participate in his life.

7. Use Scripture as needed. You may recite some or let them read the passages.

8. Remember, this is not a decision to join an organization. It is a relationship with a person, an invitation to a new life and a new community: "Come follow me."

As the person expresses the desire to follow Jesus, encourage them to read the Gospel of Mark and discover the life of Jesus and his teachings more clearly.

SESSION 1.
JESUS CONFRONTS OUR ENEMY.
Luke 8:26-39.

Encountering Jesus (15 minutes). Jesus confronts a demon-possessed man. Walter Liefeld describes common effects of demon possession ("Luke," in *Expositor's Bible Commentary*):

- disregard for personal dignity (nakedness)
- social isolation
- retreat to simple shelters (caves, tombs)
- recognition of Jesus' deity
- demonic control of speech
- shouting
- extraordinary strength

The demons, calling themselves Legion, address Jesus as the Son of the Most High God (see Daniel 3:26). With this title they acknowledge Jesus' power and deity. The demons cause the man to fall at Jesus' feet, but this is not an act of worship in the normal sense of the word. It is an act of submission; the plea "I beg you, don't torture me!" seems to be a request not to throw them into the Abyss, understood as an underworld prison for evil beings. *Legion* means "many"; the term was used to designate a Roman division of thousands of soldiers.

The pig herders seem more concerned with their business prospects than with the afflicted man. Or perhaps they are afraid of what they see—the former wild man now sitting clothed and in his right mind—and do not know what to make of Jesus. Is he a magician? A sorcerer? God? They do not know, so they'd prefer that he leave. Amazing.

The townspeople and eyewitnesses see or hear of the miracle, yet they too all join in to request Jesus' departure. They are overcome with fear. Eager at first to tell others what happened, they fall victim to crowd psychology, together thinking as one fearful person. Jesus honors their request without judgment or argument.

The demon-possessed man first sees Jesus, then cries out and falls down at Jesus' feet. We are not sure how much of his response is controlled by the demons, but we know it is the demons that speak. How much of the man is really "there" is uncertain. However, after the demons are cast out into the pigs, the man is immediately healed. He regains his mind, and he recovers his sense of dignity and is clothed.

His life has been changed, and he begs Jesus to let him come along. Perhaps he is filled with overwhelming gratitude. Instead Jesus sends him to the community where he had been living (and likely ostracized from) as a walking testimony to the power of God.

Joining the Conversation (20 minutes). The power of God does not always move people to greater devotion or submission to his authority. After the Jews were freed from Egypt, they soon grumbled and rebelled. Many saw the miracles of Christ but did not follow. After the raising of Lazarus from the dead, the religious leaders tried to have Lazarus killed because too many people were believing in Jesus!

People fear the power of God because it changes their world, moves them out of their comfort zone and pushes them to recognize who he is (and submit to his lordship). Many people fear change, and they fear being near powerful people. It is too intimidating.

Connecting Our Stories (20 minutes). We all have personal fears and hopes. We can be fickle and moody, changing our mind and attitude in a moment. We can also submit to crowd psychology, going along with what others believe even though in our heart we know they are wrong.

Help group members recognize how Jesus has confronted their enemy—the biggest being death. He has confronted the power and rule of the evil one. He has confronted sin head-on. He has probably done much more at the personal level for several people in the room. Hopefully they will recognize that and tell others about it.

Finding Our Way (10 minutes). Once again, it is important to draw on the power of community. We have trouble facing our enemies and need the help and support of Jesus and others who are in the company of Jesus.

Help members understand that they have a story to tell. The Bible is filled with stories, because stories change people. We identify with them at an emotional level, discovering common elements that inspire us and remind us of our need for God. People may think their enemy is not a significant one because it is not cancer or an abusive relationship. But the real enemy—Satan—is behind the destruction and evil in this world. He is always at work seeking to tear down what we build up. Perhaps we all simply need to be more aware of that reality.

Praying Together (about 10 minutes). Jesus prayed in John 17 for protection from the evil one. Pray for protection, strength and courage to face the battles that the world sends our way. Pray for the power of Christ to confront these enemies in his strength.

SESSION 2.
JESUS PROVIDES OUR STRATEGY.
Matthew 10:5-20.

Encountering Jesus (15 minutes). Jesus' instructions may sound severe, or at least a bit awkward, to the average ear. He wants his followers to live by faith, trusting him and the people they meet to provide for their needs. This is one of the first principles of discipleship: dependence on God to meet all our needs.

As you look carefully at Jesus' instructions, be careful not to apply all of this as prescriptive for Christians in general: these instructions were given to twelve Jewish Galilean men sent on a specific mission in a specific cultural setting. Nonetheless, if we pay attention we can glean many instructive parallels to consider and apply:

• What to take and what to leave behind: the principle of dependence and of simplicity (getting by on a little).

• What to say: remain faithful to the gospel. We do not make up our own message; we share the message of Christ.

• What to do: we are each called to carry out a ministry that uses our gifts and honors Christ.

• What to do if the message is received or rejected: trust God for results. Do not force or fabricate them. If rejected, move on. If there is openness, stay and continue to work.

- What to watch out for: be aware of the obstacles, dangers and challenges of the task God has given you. Be sober minded and not overly idealistic about ministry. It is hard, and there is opposition.
- What treatment to expect from those in power: jealousy, intimidation and possibly persecution for following Christ and proclaiming his message.
- What to say and not say when questioned: don't plan a speech, and don't worry about it; God the Holy Spirit will give you words to say, so trust him.
- What to expect in the way of a reward (see verses 40-42): God handles the rewards, and we can be assured he is just, fair and generous.

Jesus encourages the Twelve to trust the Holy Spirit and to maintain a long-term perspective that will carry them through the temporal trials of this world. Rewards lie ahead for those who rely on God and seek his ways.

Joining the Conversation (20 minutes). A good strategy outlines the objective very clearly and clarifies everyone's role in reaching the objective. Everyone has a responsibility and thus some accountability for reaching the goals together. A good strategy is achievable, not simply a pipe dream. It has measurable steps and can be evaluated along the way. A good strategy takes into account the costs of carrying out the mission, the obstacles to be overcome, and the resources available to launch and sustain the project. Success is clearly defined, and rewards are stated so that people know the payoff, in both tangible and intangible terms.

As part of his strategy Jesus tells the Twelve to go to Israel first. This is not a principle of exclusion; it is a principle of priority and compatibility. The gospel was offered to God's chosen people *first*, not *exclusively*. They had been given the Law and the Prophets, and thus they should be the most prepared to receive the gospel. Further, no plan can be accomplished all at once. You must start somewhere. The Twelve were Jewish and would be able to connect most readily with Jewish people, whose language, culture and religious heritage they were already familiar with.

Connecting Our Stories (20 minutes). As members respond, look for ways to connect their stories to each other. Often experiences in sports, scouting, work or volunteering have elements in common. You are always looking for commonalities in your group.

What kind of follower is Jesus looking for? Based on this passage, he wants people who will trust him, depend on his provision, consider the cost of discipleship, step out in faith, speak the truth in love, and be willing to accept the consequences associated with fighting spiritual battles in a hostile culture. Such followers are not casual observers, waiting to be entertained by Jesus. Rather, they put on their battle gear and prepare to engage the enemy in the power and authority of Christ.

Finding Our Way (10 minutes). To be wise as a serpent and gentle as a dove means that prudence is combined with a level of innocence. The goal is not to be so cautious and cunning as to lose one's kind disposition toward outsiders. Yet we must also avoid a mindless naiveté, assuming the best in everyone without recognizing the evil schemes of some.

Praying Together (about 10 minutes). It has been said that the kingdom of heaven is upside down compared to the world. To gain life we must lose it, to live we must die, and so on. The values seem reversed. Actually, they are right side up; it's the world's system that has things distorted. In any case, here it is wise to pray that we see the kingdom of heaven for what it is. In such prayer we align ourselves with Jesus' strategy for expanding and extending that kingdom rule into all the world.

SESSION 3.
JESUS CHOOSES OUR WEAPONS.
Mark 9:14-29.

Encountering Jesus (15 minutes). Jesus is frustrated at the disciples' lack of faith. He has already performed miracles among them and demonstrated his power. He has given them authority and power to cast out demons (Mark 3:14-15), and they had been successful at this kind of ministry already (Mark 6:12-13). So what is the problem here? The unbelieving generation is the Jews for whom Jesus has come as Messiah. They keep following Jesus but cannot seem to embrace him despite his displays of power. His rebuke is also directed at the disciples, who, as rising leaders, cannot seem to act in the faith and power Jesus has given them.

The boy is likely suffering from a kind of epilepsy that is further aggravated by a demonic spirit. This does *not* mean that everyone with epilepsy is demon possessed. In this case, the epileptic-type fit and symptoms are accompanied by a controlling force in the boy's life. He is not just sick; he is under the power of evil, and the father, the disciples and Jesus all recognize it.

Verses 23-24 are the turning point in the story. Jesus is looking for faith. He wants followers who believe in him for who he is. If they believe who he is, then they can believe in what he can do. He is testing the man's faith and honesty. The man displays both with his statement, revealing the inner struggle it costs him to trust Jesus and overcome his unbelief. The crowd is watching, and this becomes another teachable moment for Christ.

This spirit comes out by prayer, but Jesus does not pray! You'd think he would practice what he preaches. Actually, what Jesus is saying to the disciples concerns *their* unbelief and perhaps their complacency. In Mark 6:12-13 they cast out many demons. Perhaps they had become overconfident and were relying on their own power. They had stopped praying, stopped drawing strength from God. Yes, Jesus has commissioned them and given them power, but that is not a substitute for a relationship with God. They were not given a onetime megadose of spiritual strength so they can operate on their own. Prayer is still their source, and they must continue in prayer to receive fresh power, just as Jesus maintains a practice of daily prayer with his heavenly Father.

Joining the Conversation (20 minutes). The purpose of this list is to identify the current practice and understanding of prayer in your group. Don't force people to talk about what they circled, unless they seem open to do so. The point is to help people see that we are all in different places with prayer. We need to be honest about what we already do and to seek to improve in our practice of prayer and our faith in God to act. These responses may also help you when you meet individually with members. A person's prayer life is a significant indicator of their spiritual growth and their relationship with God.

Verses 23-24 are some of the most powerful in the Bible. There is power for all who believe. Yet we are not required to have full, unwavering belief in order for Jesus to act. He does not say, "Well, I'm glad you have some faith. Come back to me when all your doubts are gone, and we'll see what we can do about your son." Instead Jesus is looking for faith—it can be as small as a mustard seed as long as it is centered in him. The disciples had begun to have faith in themselves and had given up on prayer, a sign that their faith in God was diminishing.

Connecting Our Stories (20 minutes). Here you are looking for areas of potential unbelief so you can encourage people to step out in faith—even if it is just a small step of faith. It may be encouraging seekers to believe that God cares about them and wants to answer their questions. It may be helping a single person trust God with the future—career, marriage and finances.

When we hear how God has worked and is acting today, we experience great encouragement. So if there are stories of answered prayer and God's intervention, tell them and celebrate them.

Finding Our Way (10 minutes). Prayer is a weapon in our arsenal against sin and evil. Praying together is powerful, and praying persistently is evidence of our faith and our willingness to work at this discipline. We are encouraged in 1 Thessalonians 5:18 to pray continually, and that is easier when there are others to encourage us.

God's Word is another weapon. Our focus here is prayer, but read Luke 4:1-13 and remind the group that strength and power for facing evil can be drawn from the Word of God as we believe it and use it in prayer. The truth changes us and increases our confidence in prayer. Jesus was confident in the Word of God and likely meditated on it while he was in the wilderness before encountering Satan there (Matthew 4:1-11).

Praying Together (about 10 minutes). We need help to pray bold prayers. It is easy to get discouraged by ourselves. Consider asking folks to begin praying regularly with a prayer partner. You can assign members to one another, or ask if there is someone they'd like to pray with. This not only helps with some accountability but, more important, allows you to support one another and to leverage God's power in community. "Whenever two or three are gathered in my name, there I am," says Jesus.

SESSION 4.
JESUS SUPPLIES OUR STRENGTH.
Matthew 28:16-20; Acts 1:1-8.

Encountering Jesus (15 minutes). In the Great Commission in Matthew 28 Jesus draws his authority from the Father. It has been given to him—*all* authority, not some. He is God and carries all the power and authority associated with deity. He commands the disciples to go in faith and do his work. They have apostolic authority, the power of Jesus and (as we see in Acts 1) the power of the Spirit. The presence of Jesus goes with them.

Jesus has given his followers responsibility to reach the world with his life-changing message, but he gives them his presence and his power and tells them they act on his authority. They need not fear or worry.

As he had taught them earlier, Jesus had to leave in order to give the Spirit. Now he fulfills that reality, but says he will always be with them (through the Spirit). They must now trust in the invisible but real presence of Jesus Christ. He will not walk beside them, eat with them or teach them in a small group. The Holy Spirit is their teacher. They have the word of God and the power of his Spirit.

The Bible gives witness to the plurality of persons within the Godhead. Each person—the Father, Son and Spirit—possesses all the attributes of God. These include, but are not limited to, holiness, goodness, omnipotence and omniscience. Each is unchanging in nature, eternal, true, just and sinless. The Bible also affirms the oneness, or unity, of God. To hold that God is one and yet three certainly creates a mysterious tension. But if we believe the Bible to be truthful, we must embrace this tension. Our God is unique compared to all other religions. This "tri-unity" or "trinity" is a theological reality based on all the Bible teaches regarding the nature of God, coexisting as Father, Son and Spirit.

All three Persons of the Trinity are at work in this passage. The Father gives authority, the Son gives commands and promises his presence, and the Spirit acts on behalf of both as the living expression of God in us. The Spirit supplies the strength we need to be witnesses of Jesus. We are not witnesses of the Spirit. We are under the authority of the Father, we work in the power of the Spirit, and we tell the story of Jesus.

Joining the Conversation (20 minutes). The disciples are still looking for the nation of Israel to be reestablished in all its glory, but the kingdom Jesus is building goes beyond that to the entire world. They still have a Jewish-centered view of evangelism, despite the commands of Matthew 28:19-20. They are anticipating that God will exercise a political or military rule over his people. They remain unaware of God's deeper spiritual leadership over his creation. Jesus reminds them that this is for the Father to administer, not them. Their mission is different. Instead of receiving a new political realm to live in, they will receive power to live by.

Waiting for the Spirit must have been hard. Jesus is gone, they are still a bit confused, and so much has happened so quickly over the last month that their heads are probably still spinning. Now they are supposed to travel the globe telling this story.

Connecting Our Stories (20 minutes). Here you want to encourage believers to identify and fulfill their calling to be ministers of the good news. We all play a role in advancing the purposes of God together in the power of the Spirit. What does each follower of Christ know about their gifts, strengths and purpose in this life? How will they put those to work so that God is glorified? And are they going to rely on the Holy Spirit to be their source of strength? And for seekers in the group, how do they understand the nature of their gifts and abilities? Do they believe God is involved in gifting them? What do they perceive as the source of their strengths?

Finding Our Way (10 minutes). Here are some practical ways to think about acting as a group. Simply use this for ideas and discussion. It is here to prompt thinking, not to limit your possibilities.

It is not unusual to see Christians abusing the authority given them. We are not lone rangers with unlimited power and authority. We are part of a community that is to remain in submission to God, listening to the Spirit. Authority is abused when Christians try to use it to forward their own agenda or to procure material goods that serve only themselves. We must use the power we have wisely. That is why the church has elders or pastors and leaders to guide us, and little communities like small groups to help us discern what God is doing.

Prayer, the wisdom of others and the Word of God provide good checks and balances against the abuse or misuse of divine power.

Praying Together (about 10 minutes). Pray that people will understand the possibilities and limits of their power. Remind one another that God is eager through Christ to supply the strength we need, and that comes by his Spirit. Pray for power to speak the message of Christ with boldness and love. Pray that God will open your eyes to a world that needs this message. And pray for ways to serve the world around you as you demonstrate the love of Jesus.

SESSION 5.
JESUS SECURES OUR VICTORY.
John 12:20-36.

Encountering Jesus (15 minutes). Allow members a few minutes to answer this. Groups of two or three may serve the purpose well. Here are a few insights that may help as you debrief.

Jesus was aware that his death was part of the grand design of God for redemptive history. It was for this reason that he had come: to take away the sin of the world. This passage affirms that he is the Son of Man, a title of deity associated with the Old Testament designation of Messiah. His death will bring life to others. If he is crucified (lifted up), he will draw all people to himself. They will be confronted with the cross and have to choose whether to follow him.

He also sees the cross as a means of defeating the evil one and judging all those who reject him. The cross is an instrument of death. We are called to die to sin and self. But those who remain prideful and do not believe they need a savior are left with their sin-filled lives. They are already judged (John 3:16-21 is a helpful passage to read in this regard). Jesus calls himself the light (see John 9:5) and invites people to believe in him while there is time.

Jesus is certain about his death and his mission. He has come from the Father and has obeyed him. Because he is God and knows the plan of God for the salvation of people, he has a great deal of certainty.

Joining the Conversation (20 minutes). Jesus often speaks in paradoxes, and this is one of the more prominent among them: in order to gain life you must first lose it. Jesus is the model for this as well. He will die, like a grain of wheat falling to the ground, and then produce much life. We who follow him must die to pride and selfish ambition, yielding our lives to him.

Because Satan is alive and still has power in the world, sometimes the reader of this text is confused. Did Jesus defeat the evil one at the cross? If so, then why is he still free to roam? In John 17:15 Jesus prays that the Father would protect his followers from the evil one. So what actually happened at the cross?

It is clear that in Jesus Christ the kingdom of God has come to earth. It is fully available, but it has not been fully consummated (completed). The King and his power are present, but not fully. Yet Christ's defeat of the evil one is often spoken of as completed because the work is done and the victory secured (John

12:31; Colossians 2:13-15). This is often called an "already-but-not-yet" view of God's work.

Picture a large snowball rolling down a mountain toward a small house made of cardboard, getting bigger and faster as it rushes downhill. Nothing can stop it; its destination and destructive impact are assured. Once you start the snowball rolling, you can say, "That house is history! It's all over!" But in another sense, the job is not complete until gravity does its full work and the cardboard building is flattened.

Christ defeated the devil at the cross, but it will take time before the full effect is realized and completed. The full expression of the power and rule of the kingdom does not happen until the judgment is complete (Matthew 13:24-30). In this sense, Jesus is ruling over a divided kingdom: one group gives allegiance to him, while another, under the control of Satan, remains rebellious. But one day this will all change (Philippians 2:9-11; Revelation 21:1-8).

Connecting Our Stories (20 minutes). Remind your group of the spiritual forces at work in this world. The battle is won, but it is not over. So evil (restrained by the power of the Spirit and forced back by the advancing impact of the church) remains for a while. The battle is real, but the weapons of prayer and the Word of God are sufficient to fight it.

The chart is a tool for your use if it serves the group. Jesus is calling people to walk in the light, so it may be a good exercise to contrast that with walking in the darkness. The chart should prompt some thinking about how attitudes and actions change when people follow Christ (walk in the light).

Finding Our Way (10 minutes). If our victory is secure in Christ, and the evil one is defeated, how do we live? What difference does it make in our relationships and choices? Many New Testament Christians clung hard to their hope of a better life beyond the grave (Hebrews 11:13-16, 39-40). Knowing we have victory over evil and death, we rejoice in the present and have a sure hope for the future. Pain, suffering, sin and death take on new meanings: they are difficult but temporary.

Praying Together (about 10 minutes). You could lead a prayer time that begins with sentence prayers. "Dear God, I am grateful for the victory of the cross because it means . . ." Allow members to complete that sentence. Give them time to reflect silently or to write thoughts down before praying aloud.

SESSION 6.
JESUS CELEBRATES OUR TRIUMPH.
Luke 10:16-24.

Encountering Jesus (15 minutes). Jesus has just finished saying that those who listen to the disciples listen to him. That means the disciples are Jesus' representatives and spokespersons, as it were. This statement emphasizes their relationship to him—but they respond by celebrating what they have done. "Even the demons submit" seems to imply, "Yes, people listened to us, but what was really exciting was that the *demons* listened to us!" The disciples are focused on temporal things instead of eternal things. To have one's name written in heaven implies a relationship with the God of the universe. That is worth celebrating!

Jesus has given them authority to trample on snakes and scorpions and not be harmed. This is not to be taken in a literal sense, though some have tried. God's protection over them might have included a special physical blessing—we are not certain of that. If so, it did not last and was intended to be temporal: many of Jesus' followers (most notably among the Twelve) died as martyrs for their allegiance to Jesus. "Snakes and scorpions" probably refers to evil powers (the devil is a serpent in the Garden of Eden) and makes vivid to the seventy-two that they indeed have been given authority over the evil one—not invulnerability.

Jesus is enthusiastic and full of joy because of the revelation of God to his followers. The disciples have not learned the things of God through research or human wisdom; these have been revealed to them through Christ. "Little children" are those who respond to God by faith and simple trust. They are humble and willing to learn (see 1 Corinthians 1:26-29).

The prophets who spoke of Messiah and longed for his day died before their message was fulfilled. Kings who ruled in the line of David, from whose seed Messiah would come, did not seem him. But God has fully revealed himself in the person of Jesus, and the disciples are seeing this firsthand! They are indeed blessed.

Joining the Conversation (20 minutes). As a member of the seventy-two, you probably feel wonder, elation, power, joy, hope and confidence. A year ago you were just living as a fisherman or tax collector or servant or homemaker, and now you are speaking and teaching with the authority of God, healing the sick and raising the dead. You are seeing God reveal himself to you, and Messiah is walking among you!

The revelation of God is significant. He is choosing people to whom he will show himself. This should create in us a spirit of gratitude and worship. We cannot take any credit for knowing God or for having the chance to experience a relationship with Jesus Christ. We are not better or smarter than others. God has shown us himself—he has opened up the windows of heaven for us to have a glimpse of his glory in Christ. All we can do is be grateful and seek to obey his commands.

Connecting Our Stories (20 minutes). Here members can share experiences when God worked in them. Such stories are powerful, even if on the surface they seem to be insignificant. God is at work in many ways, some deep and mysterious, some simple. Tell your own story as well. It will set the tone. It does not have to be dramatic, just real. Describe real ways in which you have see God at work in you.

To be his representative is an awesome responsibility. It means we have been entrusted with a message and way of life that reflect Jesus. We should be sobered by this. It is a humbling thing, and we must remember the One we stand for. When people hear us, they hear Jesus. When people see us act, they see Jesus. We are his ambassadors and his church.

Finding Our Way (10 minutes). The fact that the harvest is plentiful is encouraging. Yes, we are sent out as sheep among wolves. There are spiritual battles and challenges. But Jesus says there is fruit out there if we just go by faith and do ministry in his name. There are people ready to become followers, people ready to be healed and encouraged, people ready to be freed from sin and shame, people ready to be taught the amazing truths of God.

Praying Together (about 10 minutes). It is very important to celebrate as a group. God is working among you. One way to do this is a group timeline. Use a large sheet of paper to lay out the number of months or years the group has met. Ask each person to mark the timeline at three or four points where the group has been an instrument of God's grace in their life. It could be when they were sick and the group prayed, or a time when a certain truth became real to them, or the day they understood saving grace. You get the idea. Then, after everyone has written on the timeline, allow time to tell stories and celebrate God's work.

Also available from InterVarsity Press and Willow Creek Resources

BIBLE 101. *Where truth meets life.*
Bill Donahue, series editor

The Bible 101 series is designed for those who want to know how to study God's Word, understand it clearly and apply it to their lives in a way that produces personal transformation. Geared especially for groups, the series can also profitably be used for individual study. Each guide has five sessions that overview essential information and teach new study skills. The sixth session brings the skills together in a way that relates them to daily life.

FOUNDATIONS: *How We Got Our Bible*
Bill Donahue

TIMES & PLACES: *Picturing the Events of the Bible*
Michael Redding

COVER TO COVER: *Getting the Bible's Big Picture*
Gerry Mathisen

STUDY METHODS: *Experiencing the Power of God's Word*
Kathy Dice

INTERPRETATION: *Discovering the Bible for Yourself*
Judson Poling

PARABLES & PROPHECY: *Unlocking the Bible's Mysteries*
Bill Donahue

GREAT THEMES: *Understanding the Bible's Core Doctrines*
Michael Redding

PERSONAL DEVOTION: *Taking God's Word to Heart*
Kathy Dice